Characters Through the Ages

Book Three

Watching David and Goliath

Growing in faith
God Bless
Jean W Martin
12-25-16

Endorsements

Jann Martin knows how to write for kids! She combines imagination with adventure to create a chapter book that children will love. Young readers will enjoy traveling with Sarah and Daniel in their homemade time machine. In this first book of the series, readers will travel to the very beginning of time to meet Adam in the garden. Bible facts and lessons are gently woven into the story, and discussion questions at the end of the book will stimulate young minds. Once kids read this book, they well be eager for the next.

—**Crystal Bowman**, bestselling children's author

Jann Martin's most recent literary effort for children, *Bible Characters Through the Ages—Adam in the Garden,* is a compelling read for people of any age. Jann has the ability to enter into the imaginary world of a child while at the same moment appealing to those of us who are grown to allow us to return to the world we experienced growing up where "all things are possible."

From the earliest pages where the children, Daniel and Sarah, begin to imagine and to plan for "time travel," throughout their time excursion into the world of early Genesis and back home again, not wishing their parents to worry about them, the plot line pulls you eagerly forward.

While reading, I couldn't help but entertain the thought, "What if …?" Then, I suddenly realized reading Biblical traditions in a fresh and engaging way is actually like becoming a "time traveler" in a sense, where the promises of the past come alive in the present.

—Pastor Drex Morton,
St. John's Lutheran Church, Bridgewater, MI

Jann's writing will definitely keep children coming back for more. The lively language and fun element of time travel is engaging. Readers will feel a part of the story as her two main characters experience bible stories firsthand. I'm so glad this is the first in a series because readers will be waiting for the next story with great anticipation!

—Michelle Medlock Adams,
award-winning author of over forty children's books

Bible Characters Through the Ages

Book Three

Watching David and Goliath

Jann W. Martin

Elk Lake
PUBLISHING™

Elk Lake Publishing
Bible Stories Through the Ages Book Three:
Watching David and Goliath

Requests for information should be addressed to:
Elk Lake Publishing, Atlanta, GA 30024
ISBN-13 Number: 978-1-944430-09-2

Graphics Design: Anna M. O'Brien
Editor: Deb Haggerty

Published in Association with SuzyQ Inc.

NKJV

Other Books by Jann W. Martin

Bible Characters Through the Ages Book One: Adam in the Garden

Bible Characters Through the Ages Book Two: Meeting Eve

This Babe So Small: A Story of the Nativity **1** *Samuel 17*

Prolog

In their playroom, Sarah and Daniel were standing next to Yahweh's Express, the time travel machine they made with their mom from a refrigerator box. They had the box set up with pillows to sit on, a camping lantern for light, and a dial to turn to the name of the character they wanted to visit. Above the dial was a picture looking down on a forest, so they were seemingly flying over the trees.

Chapter 1

"Daniel, who do you want to go see in Yahweh's Express next?" asked Sarah.

Daniel said, "I want to see David and Goliath. It would be cool to see the battle between them."

"That doesn't sound fun to me," Sarah frowned. "I don't like to see people get hurt. Guess you should see the characters you like, and I'll get to see some I like too."

Daniel laughed. "You pick the next one. Hurry up so we can get going."

They put their dishes in the dishwasher, then ran to the playroom and ducked inside their homemade time machine, Yahweh's Express.

"What are you bringing Princess for?" asked Daniel.

Sarah hugged her ballerina doll. "She'll bring me comfort if I get scared."

"First, we should pray and ask God if we can go to visit David." Grabbing Sarah's hand, he prayed, "Dear God, I'd like to meet David and watch him when he kills Goliath.

Sarah's not as excited to see them fight, but I told her she could pick the next one. Amen."

They were both very quiet and listened to see if they could hear an answer from God.

"I just heard a voice in my head," said Daniel. "It said, 'David's in the field with his sheep.'"

Sarah laughed. "I like the idea of meeting David with sheep instead of with a giant."

They closed their eyes, and Daniel prayed again, "We're ready, God. Let's go."

In a few moments, they felt Yahweh's Express gently land on the ground.

Sarah climbed out first this time. "Look, it's very pretty here. There are a few trees and a lot of open fields. I can see David sitting in the shade under one of the trees. He doesn't look very big. Let's go meet him."

She took off running with Daniel right behind her. David saw them coming, stood up and waved at them.

Chapter 2

"Hello, I'm David. What are your names?"

"I'm Sarah, and he's my brother, Daniel. God let us come to meet you. Can I pet one of your lambs?"

"Sure," said David. "This little one is very friendly. She loves to cuddle."

Sarah sat down, and the lamb crawled up on her lap. "The wool feels spongy and very thick. It's also slippery."

"That's the oil in the hair. The thick wool also gets a lot of twigs and grass stuck in it," said David. "If it gets wet, it takes a long time to dry. While you hold her, you can pick out the grass and twigs. That would be a big help for me."

"I would love to do that for you. What do you do all day when you are out here with the sheep?" asked Sarah.

"I play my lyre. I sing songs of praise to God and thank Him for all He has done for me," said David.

"What's a lyre?" Sarah asked.

He reached down. "This is my lyre."

"It looks like a small harp." said Sarah. "Will you please

play me something?"

"Sure. I wrote this song for God the other day."

The LORD is my shepherd; I shall not want.
He makes me to lie down in green pastures;
He leads me beside the still waters.[3]He restores my soul;
He leads me in the paths of righteousness
For His name's sake. Yea, though I walk through the valley
of the shadow of death,
I will fear no evil;
For You are with me;
Your rod and Your staff, they comfort me.
You prepare a table before me in the presence of my enemies;
You anoint my head with oil;
My cup runs over. Surely goodness and mercy shall follow me
All the days of my life;
And I will dwell in the house of the LORD Forever.[1]

"I know those words. Mom read that to me the other day. I love it. You wrote it?" asked Sarah.

"Yes. God has done so much for me; I like to write songs and sing them for Him," replied David.

"We sing songs in church and Sunday school," said Daniel. "It's fun to sing those songs. Do you like to watch over the sheep?"

1 Psalm 23, New King James Version

"I love it," said David. "It's so quiet out here in the fields most of the time. Sometimes, I have to chase away a lion or bear. Once, a lion had a little lamb in its mouth. I had to hit the lion on the head with my staff until she opened her mouth and the lamb fell to the ground."

Daniel asked "Then what did you do?"

Chapter 3

"I yelled and swung my staff and chased her away. The poor lamb was shaking and crying. I picked her up and held her for a long time. Once she stopped shaking, I put her on my shoulders and walked back to where the rest of the flock was. The rest of the day she stayed right by my side."

"Cool," said Daniel.

Sarah said. "You have a pretty important job. It sounds scary sometimes too."

"Yeah, it can be, but I wouldn't trade it for anything. Out here my older brothers can't pester me. They always think they are better than me just because they are older."

"I know what you mean," Sarah said looking at Daniel. "He thinks, because he's older, he is supposed to boss me around."

"It's just because I don't want you to get hurt," said Daniel.

"Whatever!" Sarah said, then turning to David, "Where are your brothers?"

"They're with King Saul. Our army's getting ready to fight the Philistine army. It's not too far from here," said David.

Sarah said, "Why are they going to fight?"

"Because they want the rule over the same area of land," said David. "My dad wants me to go tomorrow to see if they need anything. Would you like to go?"

"Sure," said Daniel.

Sarah backed up a step. "Oh, that sounds really scary. I would be afraid to go where they are."

"Not me." Standing tall, Daniel puffed up his chest. "I would love to go there."

"First, I have to take the sheep to the pen," said David.

"Can we help you?" asked Sarah.

"You can walk with me, but the dogs do a lot of the work keeping the sheep together," said David. "This black and white dog is Shadow; the brown spotted one is Lady,"

"How do they help you with the sheep?" asked Sarah.

"Shadow runs out in front of the sheep to show them the way. Then Lady keeps the ones in the back from staying behind. I call out to the dogs to let them know where I want them to go. We make a great team.

"Let's get started. I will introduce you to my dad, and we can have dinner," said David.

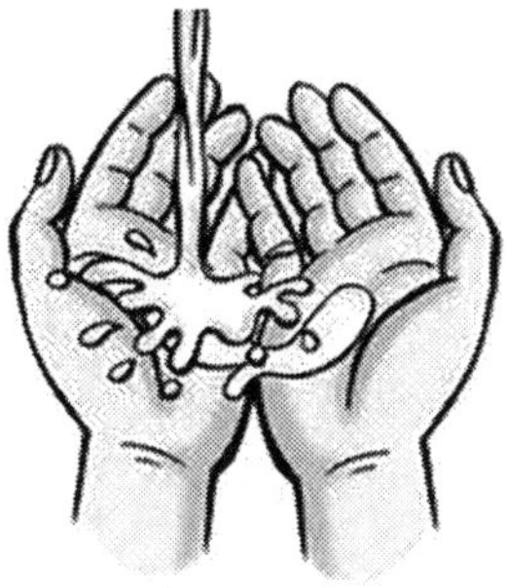

Chapter 4

Once all of the sheep were safely in their pen, David said, "Let's go to the well so we can wash our hands and then have dinner."

David pulled up a bucket of fresh water, held out a bowl and handed it to Sarah.

"What's that for?"

"It's oil and ash mixed together to clean your hands. Then you rinse them with the water in the bucket. Here comes my father now."

"Hello, Father. I would like you to meet my new friends," said David. "This is Daniel and Sarah. This is my father, Jesse."

Daniel stood very tall. "Hello, sir, it's a pleasure to meet you."

"Yes," said Sarah. "David has been showing us how to take care of the sheep. I got to hold one on my lap. She was so cuddly."

"It's very nice to meet you two. Did you all wash your hands for dinner?" Jesse asked.

"Yes, Father. We are ready to have our dinner."

They all walked in and sat on the floor around the table. There was bread, cucumbers, beans, grapes, almonds, figs, cheese, and fish.

"Wow, this looks so good," said Sarah.

"Yeah, I'm starved," said Daniel.

"First, we have to pray," said Jesse. He lowered his head. "Dear Father God, we thank you for keeping us safe today. Please bless this food to nourish our bodies and keep us strong for You. Amen."

When the platters were empty, David went and got his flute. "I'll play you some of my favorite songs."

When David was done, Jesse said, "Thank you. I always enjoy hearing you play your music. You all need to get some sleep. Tomorrow will be a busy day. I need you to take some things to your brothers, David, and see how they are doing."

"That will be awesome. I can't wait to see the army," said Daniel.

"I'm not as excited as my brother. But I'll go with them," said Sarah.

"I'll keep you safe, Sarah. Come with me, I'll show you where I sleep," David walked toward the other end of the house and took them into a large room with mats on the floor.

"This is where we all sleep. Sarah, please take my mat, you'll be more comfortable. Daniel and I will sleep on the floor.

Chapter 5

They were up early the next morning and had a quick breakfast. David gathered the food and supplies his father wanted him to take to his brothers.

"Do you have all of the supplies your brothers will need?" asked Jesse.

"Yes, Father. I have the supplies for them and food and drink for the three of us," said David.

"You better get started," said Jesse. "Walking to where the army is camped will take most of the morning. You should stay there for the night so you don't have to walk back home in the dark."

"Okay, Father. We'll see you tomorrow." He turned to Daniel and Sarah, "Are you two ready to go?"

"Yeah, let's go," said Daniel.

"I guess so," said Sarah. She held on tight to Princess, her ballerina doll.

The morning was sunny and cool when they began their walk. Along the way, they passed land being farmed. David waved to one of his friends on the other side of the field.

"What's planted in the farmers' fields?" asked Sarah.

David said, "This field is barley. Some of the other fields are wheat, vegetables, and fruit."

"What kind of fruit do you have?" asked Daniel.

"We grow grapes, pomegranates, and figs. They are sweet and are good after a meal or for a snack out in the field," said David.

"We like those fruits too," said Sarah. "They are a good snack in the afternoon."

"We better keep walking. I need to get these supplies to the camp where my brothers are," said David.

"Where are the armies?" asked Daniel.

David adjusted the food sack on his shoulder. "The Philistines are on the hill at Socoh in Judah and our army is on the hill in Elah Valley. There is big field between the two hills. That's probably where they will have the big fight."

Sarah frowned. "I'm starting to get scared; I'm not sure I really want to go through with this."

"Don't worry; this is going to be really cool," said Daniel. "David and I are here, and we will keep you safe. I thought you brought Princess to make you feel better."

"I'm holding her but this time, she's not helping very much," said Sarah.

"Look, I can see our army up ahead," David pointed.

"My three brothers, Eliab, Abinadab and Shammah, are with the group of men on the right by the tent. They look like they are getting ready to go and fight. Let's get these supplies over to them quickly."

Chapter 6

As the three of them ran up to the group of men, Abinadab, a tall muscular man called out, "Hello, little brother! I see you brought us some more supplies. Thank you. We are getting very low on food. Who is this you brought?"

"These are my friends, Daniel and Sarah," said David. "God let them come here to meet us. They are very interested in what we are doing. They have never seen an army before."

Another of David's brothers walked over to greet them. "What did you bring us today?" asked Shammah.

"Dad gave me a sack of cracked wheat and loaves of bread for you and ten wedges of cheese for your captain."

"That sounds great," said Abinadab. "Put them in the tent; we have to get going."

Just as David came back out of the tent, he saw a huge man—really, he looked like a giant— stomping across the field.

"Who is that huge guy?" asked David.

"That's Goliath." said Abinadab. "He's about ten feet

tall. His helmet is made of bronze, and look at all of that armor! The armor looks like it would weigh over one hundred pounds. He also has bronze shin guards and a sword. That sword looks like one of the rails in our fence. The tip alone looks like it weighs fifteen pounds. Another man ahead of him is holding his shield, which looks heavy too."

Shammah narrows his eyes. "He has come to us before. He says the same thing every time." "Listen, here he goes again."

> *Why have you come out to line up for battle? Am I not a Philistine, and you the servants of Saul? Choose a man for yourselves, and let him come down to me. If he is able to fight with me and kill me, then we will be your servants. But if I prevail against him and kill him, then you shall be our servants and serve us." And the Philistine said, "I defy the armies of Israel this day; give me a man, that we may fight together.*[2]

"What do you think you are doing here?" The voice behind them made Sarah, Daniel and David jump.

"Hi, Eliab," David started to say, but his brother cut him off.

"You probably came just to get in the way and see the

2 1 Kings 17:8-10, New King James Version.

battle. And you brought these two. You better make them stay way back by the tent."

"Yes, I agree; they should stay by the tent. But I have a right to be here too. I'm going to go and see if I can talk to King Saul."

His brothers laughed. Eliab said, "Sure, what do you think you can do!"

David ignored him and walked over to King Saul's tent. Daniel and Sarah quietly followed. When they got to the tent, David turned to them.

"Wait out here; I need to talk with the king alone," said David.

Daniel stood tall and brave, but Sarah was shaking and holding onto Princess as tight as she could.

The king's servant asked King Saul if David could come in and talk with him.

"Come on, Sarah," whispered Daniel. "Let's see if we can hear what the king says."

"You listen," said Sarah. "I'm waiting right here."

Daniel leaned in close to the tent to overhear.

"Yes, let him in," said King Saul. "Hello, boy, what are you doing out here?"

"I came to bring some supplies from my father, Jesse, to my brothers," said David.

"Well, that's good of you, son. Now you need to head back home before the fighting begins. You are too young to be out here."

"The others all backed away from Goliath. I am not afraid of him," David said. "I want a chance to kill him. I have killed lions trying to take our sheep. I know I can do this. I know God will be with me and help me."

"Go, then, and may God protect you," said King Saul. "Here you can wear my armor."

David put on the king's armor—a heavy bronze helmet and coat of metal. He stumbled under the heavy weight. Then picking up the sword, he fell to the floor. "I can't go in this armor; it weighs too much." Letting go of the sword, he pushed himself up on his knees. First, he took off the heavy helmet, then, struggling, he pulled off the metal coat. Standing again, he grabbed his staff and left the king's tent.

Chapter 7

Standing tall, David said, "Come with me. I need to go over to the brook."

"What do you need from the brook?" asked Sarah.

David bent down and picked up five smooth stones, each as big as his fist, and put them in his bag.

"What do you need stones for?" asked Daniel.

"They are for me to use against Goliath," said David.

"How can stones help you?" asked Sarah.

"I can use stones as a weapon. God told me He would give me His power when I use this tool in His name," said David. "I have used them to kill lions when they are coming after my sheep."

"Oh, my, that sounds so scary." Sarah held Princess even tighter.

"Nah, it's really easy and I haven't missed yet. You two stay here; I don't want you to be too close."

David lifted his head high and started toward Goliath.

"Who's this boy?" asked Goliath. "He doesn't look like

he could kill a fly. You think he is going to stop me?"

"I am David. I come to you in the name of God, the God of Israel's armies. With the power of God, I will defeat you."

"So you think this God will help you? Let's see what you've got."

Daniel and Sarah walked a little closer, but still stayed behind some of the Israelite soldiers.

David stood as tall as he could and spoke to Goliath. "You come with a sword and a spear. I come in the name of the Lord, the God of Israel. God will deliver you into my hand."

David reached into his bag, pulled out one of the stones and put it in his sling.

Goliath looked down at David. "You really think you can stop me with that little toy?"

David stood taller, swung his arm around several times, aimed the sling at Goliath's head and let the stone fly. Suddenly the earth shook as Goliath fell to the ground. He died as soon as the stone struck him.

Afraid, Goliath's men ran away as fast as they could go.

Walking toward David, Daniel exclaimed, "Wow, that was awesome!"

Sarah said, "Yeah, you really are strong,"

"It's not by my power, but by God's amazing grace I can protect myself and those around me." David looked at the king's tent. "I need to go see King Saul."

"We should head back home," said Sarah.

"Thanks for letting us spend time with you," said Daniel.

Sarah and Daniel turned, walked a few steps to go behind a tent and prayed, asking for Yahweh's Express to come for them. Then, just a short distance away, their craft appeared behind some trees.

"That ended up pretty cool," said Sarah. "I can't wait to tell Mom and Dad about this.

"Who do you want to visit next?" asked Daniel.

"I'm not sure. I'll have to think about it." Sarah looked back. David seemed to be getting smaller as he walked away.

Discussion Questions

Chapter 1

1. Would you want to meet David and Goliath? Why or why not?
2. Do you have something like Sarah's doll that makes you feel stronger?
3. Have you ever been to a field where the sheep are eating?
4. What do you think it would be like to stay out in the field all of the time like a shepherd?

Chapter 2

5. Would you want to hold a lamb?
6. Have you seen a lyre? Do you play an instrument?
7. Do you have a favorite Bible verse? What is your favorite song to sing at church?
8. How did you feel when you read the part about David chasing away the lion?

Chapter 3

9. Do you think you could calm a scared lamb? What would you do?
10. Do you have brothers and sisters? Are you the oldest? Who thinks they are always in charge?
11. Would you want to go watch two armies fight? Why or why not?

12. Do you think keeping the sheep together to take them to their pen would be hard?

Chapter 4

13. Have you ever heard of washing your hands with ash and oil?
14. What do you think about sitting on the floor to eat your dinner?
15. Do you do things together as a family after dinner?
16. What do you think about your whole family sleeping in the same room on mats?

Chapter 5

17. Have you ever seen a farmer's field? What was growing in it?
18. Have you ever grown any food?
19. How would you feel as you walked up to the hills where the armies were?
20. Do you think seeing David's brothers made Sarah feel better?

Chapter 6

21. What would your first reaction be at seeing Goliath?
22. Do you think David was brave to want to fight Goliath?
23. Would you have gone to the king to tell him you wanted a chance to fight Goliath?
24. Do you think you could wear the king's armor?

Chapter 7

25. Have you ever used a sling?
26. Do you think a sling and stone is a good weapon to use against a giant?
27. Why would getting hit in the head cause Goliath to die?
28. David said that God's power was what killed Goliath. Has God given you strength to do something you didn't think you could do?

About the Author

Jann W. Martin—author, teacher, speaker, and blogger. Her dream is to capture the hearts of children by writing stories teaching them the Bible through the eyes of a child. She has a BA in Early Elementary Education from Michigan State University (1972) and is a retired Commissioned Associate in Ministry from Trinity Lutheran Seminary (1999). She served at two congregations writing curriculum for children and adults on several different topics.

Her first published book (2007), "This Babe So Small," the nativity told through the eyes of the innkeeper's daughter, has sold over 2,000 copies. After moving to Florida, she found the Word Weavers writing group. They have supported and encouraged her to write for older children, which resulted in "Bible Characters Through the Ages." Writing has opened her heart and mind to seeing the Bible stories in a fresh new way.

You can join her at www.jannwmartin.com

39549625R10022

Made in the USA
San Bernardino, CA
29 September 2016